SOCIAL MEDIA MARKETING FOR BEGINNERS

A brief guide for beginner's to market their ventures and campaigns.

Vardhane Harsh

Social Media Marketing for beginners
By Vardhane Harsh
Copyright © 2013 Vardhane Harsh
2nd Edition
ISBN: *1490935711*

ISBN 13 : *978-1490935713*

To

Grandpa and Grandma

I am from you and I will be from you

Introduction

Hey guys , Do you see the change coming? Don't you see how technology has reshaped the whole scheme of marketing?

With more than 300 million people active facebookusers,more than 350 million bloggers, more than 100 million viewers on youtube and nearly 20 million twitter users

Do you still believe that the old medium of marketing like ads in TV and Newspapers are still effective? Ofcourse No.

Today with the power of Social Media, you don't need to spend money marketing your ventures. Just sitting at your own comfort, You can market anything through Facebook,twitter,youtube,blogger and many more social tools and reach a very large audience and customer base. New web technologies have made it easy for anyone to create—and, most importantly—distribute their own content. A blog post, tweet, or YouTube video can be produced and viewed by millions virtually for free. Advertisers don't have to pay publishers or distributors huge sums of money to spread their messages.now they can make their own interesting content that viewers will flock to.

The following book is a guide to beginner's probably the new age College students Who don't understand social media marketing and would like to learn its basics to use it to market their ventures.

Contents

Have A Hub..

Selection of social sites

Link the profiles

Time for Some Viral Marketing !!

Viral marketing

Gambling on campaigns and ventures

Nothing is sure to get Viral

Thank you,

Aknowledgements

Social Media Marketing –WHY?

Why is everyone doing this? Because its easier to communicate a message via social media tools.

Why send you a letter in the mail when I can get you to subscribe to my blog and get all news updates (or email for that matter)? Why spend millions on TV advertising when I can really get you too look by posting incredible deals on Facebook and new videos on YouTube?

The biggest advantage of social media is clear: you get more business.
What kind of business will you get? How much can you make? And how many customers are we really talking about?

Social media encompasses the entire world, and will soon be used by everyone with a computer at least a few times a week. Facebook, as of this writing, has over 300 million people active, sharing words and pictures. From MNCs to Rural villages of India, It has got active users. There are millions of blogs online, and millions using RSS (Really Simple Syndication) read them.

How much can you make? There is No limit. One advantage was mentioned early. Why go all out in a magazine or newspaper ad which will reach a small market when you can click the mouse and send 100,000 potential customers a friendly message? And this isn't just an email we're talking about—Facebook and blogs are quite popular for posting and subscribing—so the opportunity is immense!!.

So, got an idea how powerful the Social media is?

Lets Learn How to use it to market your ventures.

Blogging

What is a Blog?

Well A blog is a platform to show your articles to the World But you will also have variety of features Like comments etc.
Your posts will have subscriptions which will make it Ideal for marketing .Blog can also be used as a Hub. A centre for all your other social media which you are using for marketing. And the best thing is that all this can be interlinked very easily.

I recommend every marketer to have a blog so that adequate communication can exist between his audience. Blogs are conversational So Don't prefer Public releases or Press releases on them.

Every time you do something good or the campaign or product achieves something ,Post about it instantly. Blog is one of the most effective marketing tool as Besides being able to spread the word about your brand quickly and easily, maintaining a blog gives you an informal way of connecting with,
listening to, responding to, and engaging in conversation with your target audience.

How To Use your Blog

Surely Blogging can give high profits due to its high potential but some risks are also involved. A large number of businesses and ventures are going into marketing without a proper plan for Blogging or some other social media tools. They Push up a good website with some ads, even trying Search engine optimization(SEO) but they fail .Why?

They don't have a planned social media compaign.They just create a blog for the sake of creating it.They just describe their business asking us to buy without giving us the reason WHY we should buy it? anybody can go to Twitter, or Facebook, and especially Wordpress, and post what they are doing. For businesses, however, things get more complicated.

"Blogging is easy! Anyone can blog!" No, it's not always easy. Actually, it's easier to set up a Twitter account and start posting text rather than publishing a blog post. But with one little blog you can reach thousands if not millions more people/customers.

Let me tell you how you can make profit from a small blog.

You need a Provider

There is the big three of Wordpress, Blogger, and Livejournal, but for businesses your blogging providers should come down to Wordpress and Blogger. Wordpress is best for newcomers, but there are distinct differences between a free Wordpress blog and a free Blogger blog.
It depends on what you want. For instance, Blogger allows you to post ads,namely Google Adsense for free. On the other hand, Wordpress does not. However, if you choose to buy a domain name and host your Wordpress blog on its own server, which is reasonable, you can post as many ads as you want. And Wordpress, with so many options and such an easy interface, wins out in this case.
Blogger is very good too. It's simple and you can even, if you so desire, make money online passively.
However, Wordpress is the #1 in this case.

But writing the blog isn't going to bring readers to you.well you will have to pay attention to the SEO. Let's see How to apply a great SEO.

Applying a SEO

Apart from writing a great Blog, The writer of the Blog should pay concentrated attention to SEO strategy too. The blog needs to be keyword rich so people just don't find it when they type in the exact business or topic your blog is on. A keyword rich Blog will ensure more views and pay per clicks thus allowing you to earn from ads too.

For an example- If your Blog is about your college's cultural fest. But the passes are high priced; you might think a blog is worthless. However, if you make the whole field interesting, if you focus a blog on the advantages of your cultural fest over cheap ones, you might notice a difference in sale of your passes. And it may not be immediate. While your blog gets readers, hopefully it will get ranked too, and if you get the right SEO blogger, ranked highly.

.

What should be your content?

Of course you need to choose a topic of which you are a master. Now if you are choosing a topic on which there are already hundreds of blogs then it will be quiet difficult to get a good traffic. blogging is a personal medium, so focus on bringing your own voice and unique point of view forward.
Once you've picked your audience or topics, Put your efforts. Mix up the kind of content you post, emphasis on every content assuring if it will be able to drive traffic or not.

Don't Just tell stories

Blogging isn't always fun, but most people blog to just tell stories Just telling stories about your daily life incidents doesn't makes you a great blogger. Your blogging talent is identified by how much people are coming to your blog to enjoy your writings or how many products you are able to sell through your business blog. But even in the early stages of design and development you need to remember most people go online to have some fun. So keep it real!!

Let's market using social sites..

Tweet-Twitter

Twitter is a social tool which allows you to blog but this time the size of each post is limited. The maximum limit of characters is only 140.

But,

Rather than being a Limitation, It has created a new niche .It started becoming popular with high profile celebrities and today almost every celebrity is followed by their millions of fans on twitter.

I recommend using twitter mostly to promote your new blog posts etc. It requires very little investment of time , It is much efficient than traditional Blogging.

How Marketers can use it?

Hashtags

Terms with # sign are called hashtags. If someone uses a hashtag in a post and the tag when clicked by another person shows him all the relevant tweets with that hashtag.I prefer its better to go with a single or maximum 2 hashtags so that you don't distract your audience more to your hashtag in place of your link.

Retweet

When someone likes your tweet and shares it with his/her followers then it's called a retweet. When you hover over a tweet in Twitter, you'll see the option to retweet. Most Twitter management tools will allow you to retweet any tweets you see as well.

Hat Tip

A hat tip is like a user credit given by one user to another on discovering something.for instance you decide to share some blog post without retweeting its original user, Credit can still be given to them with a HT@username.

Trends

Same as Hot news,Twitter has ongoing Hot Topics which are based on keywords and hashtags.To get more exposure tweet

Mention

 When your username is used in a tweet ,The person using it mentions you with @username

Follow Important people

I recommend you to follow all those important people who are somehow related to your campaign or venture or are masters in the field f your campaign etc. There knowledge can always be helpful.

Facebook for Marketing

Facebook is the king of social media, even if Twitter is gaining in popularity. There are over 300 million potential customers. It's free. You can both upload pictures and chat via text with clients. While it's a more chat oriented social media tool like Twitter, Facebook's sheer size makes it impossible to ignore.

Used in tandem with other social media tools is putting money in the book. Sign up is free, chat with clients, find new business, and find out what your customers truly want. Now Facebook has reached everywhere that simply means our message or marketing can reach anywhere where Facebook has got a presence.

Pages

We all know what a Facebook page is. If you decide to create a Facebook page for your business, don't assume that everyone will want to become a fan of it just because they know your brand or even because they've stumbled across your page by accident. Since any business can create a page on Facebook, you will be competing with hundreds or even thousands of other pages in your industry alone.
To get along this competition, you need to give something to them which will force them to Like your page.

When you're setting up a page for your business, you can use a few applications to make the page more interesting to visitors and make them more likely to return.

Your venture should have a blog to keep customers and clients updated regarding product releases or events and other news. Make sure it has an RSS feed. Use this application to pull posts from your blog onto your Facebook page.

LinkedIn-only business

LinkedIn is known as a networking and recruitment site; however, It can be used effectively by marketers too. There are now over 225m registered LinkedIn members, including 75m in the US and 50m in Europe.

Probably LinkedIn is a cornerstone for new age marketers.

For marketers, The most effective feature to use can be Answers or groups. Regular sharing of good content which will be valuable for people in that industry can also be highly beneficial.

Groups

Marketers can use groups where they feel their audience mostly is active or hangs out. By joining such groups and giving quality answers to the questions can spread the word about you and your venture.

Recommendations

Maybe it may not be the way you like but recommendations are also beneficial in marketing. Always ask people to recommend your venture or company etc on LinkedIn as in future It will improve your credibility.

Lastly I will recommend you to ask your friends and family to like and share your content repeatedly in discussions.

Marketing using Media

Multimedia sites like youtube,flickr etc can be extensively used to market your campaign or venture.today with a variety of capturing devices like camera,camcorder,mobile phones along with high speed internet ,it's just a minute game to capture something and share it to the world.

Millions of users can be easily reached by uploading videos on youtube. These days no expertise in needed in uploading a video . The added benefit is that a variety of features like sharing comments etc makes it more easy for marketers to interact with audience.

Marketers can create videos with very little expertise and upload them to YouTube to reach millions of users.

Let's talk about some of these media sharing sites-

Youtube

You might have wondered How youtube turned out to be a phenomenon for PSY or Kolaveri Di.Youtube is something which can be like Alladin's lamp for your campaign where if your video is getting views then your job's done. marketers use YouTube to host 'channels'. These channels can take a brand from being unidimensional, as presented in advertisements, to being fleshed out personalities with varied content.

Make a channel

Make your Channel with a good URL which also depends on how good username you got for your channel. Your Channel can be customized in a variety of ways so try customizing it in a way which matches the venture or campaign you are marketing.

Content

Noone on youtube want to see branded content ie ads etc.What viewers want is some videos which they will like and will comment on them.Probably if its too good then also they will Discuss and Share it on their social networking pages.
I recommend all the marketers to make their promotional video very unique and entertaining along with a shorter duration.

How should be your Videos?

Ask yourself which videos attract you and which doesn't?
The videos with a catchy title, short duration and of course an attractive thumbnail.

Videos should be of less duration as Multitasking for the viewer is not possible while exclusively watching your video.

Your thumbnail should also be something which relates to your video as it is the first exposure of your video a viewer will have.

Flickr

Flickr offers photo sharing and related services for users for all level like beginners to pro's.Its a website owned by yahoo and is easy to use .

A Flickr account can be created easily without any cost. You can sign up just using your Yahoo! ID.once joined, adding photos is a cakewalk through the very simple upload system. There are also Flickr groups which you can join but beware of their rules about pic posting. Most Flickr members are active in groups. Groups are where like-minded users post photos related to the group's theme.

Let's talk about Flickr marketing

The terms of use of Flickr clearly state that It is not to be used for any commercial purpose but Rules always have loopholes so you are just going to use your Flickr profile to tell about your campaign, product etc. .you are not asking anyone to buy it but just sharing some pics which may attract viewers attention in your product or campaign.

In your describe yourself section, write what your campaign is about or what advantage your product has but never talk about selling it or any type of sales report.

Find and join appropriate Groups

Groups is a powerful marketing tool which can be used in Flickr.

There are groups for everything. Run a car garage? There will be numerous groups on cars. Love pets? A plenty of groups on pets.
Just join any group which relates to your campaign or product and when appropriate, Start posting photos and participating in discussions so that your venture along with you can reach an audience.

Use unique and attractive text for each photo

You can write a description for each photo you upload along with giving it a unique name. The description should be accurate and again should not sound like you are trying to sell it.

Tags can also be added in these photos so add adequate tags which are relevant to your photo and the audience to which you want to market .

Lastly Don't plaster your url everywhere unnecessarily and never post any advertising message in discussion groups.

SlideShare

SlideShare is one of the highest-traffic sites on the Internet, receiving approx 50 million unique visitors every month. It gives sheer exposure to your potential audience and SlideShare credibility for search engines.

In slideshare you can insert any presentation along with videos and a recorded audio track thus ultimately creating an audiovisual presentation.

Slideshare provides an easy platform to share digital content like word documents,powerpoint presentations and HD videos.

How to Market

Identify the people in your key networks who have a SlideShare account and be proactive in reaching out to them there.

A lot of people don't always put in the time and effort to find out who they are connected with on Twitter, Facebook or LinkedIn.
The more content you add, the more visibility you generate, which will lead to more views.
Bloggers with very good content on their blogs can use to market them by sharing content which will have a capturing lead to their blogs or ventures.

Forums

Forums can be effectively used for marketing your campaigns or product.Generally people who use forums are kinda net techies or enthusiasts and thus don't repend from online purchases. Many forum users are also respected experts and bloggers in the specific topics covered by the forum.
If through a Forum you are able to make an astounding impression in front of these techies then surely they will help you market far and wide.

Forums and Marketing
For marketing First you will have to find the right forums where the exact community is there who will be audience for your

marketing and potential buyers will lie among them.Forums with 1000 members and 10000 posts are preferred.

Make your user account and start taking part in discussions.In your signature use the URL for your blog or the campaign or product you are marketing. make valuable contributions to the community and become a valued member so that later when you suggest /market your product,your words will have weight to bind them to check it.

Social Media is just a marketing tool But It cannot replace Marketing Strategy

Lets talk about Marketing Strategy…

What Social Media gives us

Voice

Social media gives us a Voice.
Although some organisations these days have strict policies against blogging   about that organisation but Can they stop you? No.Never.
You can blog about your interests,passions anything..

Audience

Social media gives you an audience . Instead of waiting for mainstream media to determine whether your thoughts are worthy of a larger audience, you have the chance to build an audience from day one.
(And believe me, there is someone for everyone out there.)

Flexibility

Social media gives you flexibility . Are you better in pictures?
Use Flickr. Not very tech savvy? Use Utterli.
A budding Kubrick? Make a video blog. Hemingway?
Write a blog.
Social media gives you a world audience .

The strategy

Beginning

Just make a note what all social tools you are going to use.
Just don't start making accounts and facebook pages without
any strategy as it will only result in failure.
A strategy will help you ensure that you can measure your
success without getting stunned. Your compaign should be Fun.

Who is your audience??

Determining who is your audience is a tough job and its
segmentation really takes a hard work.

You have to segment your audience based on their age,character,location etc.

You will have to ask yourself that What will drive that audience to listen to your message/marketing and get convinced to follow you.

Here are some check points You will need to answer -

- Which audience you specifically want to focus on?
- Why your audience needs to know about your venture?
- Why will your audience buy your idea?
- Are you getting leads that the audience may be interested in your venture?

Only proceed after you have got suitable answers to these questions.

What are your goals?

You should clearly define the goals of your marketing strategy.setting them in advance will help keep your social media team accountable and may increase your chances of success. A strong unified approach helps you shape the strategy for each section of audience you are targeting for marketing your ventures.

Your goals can be generating more traffic for your website or blog.
It can also be increasing your brand exposure by getting more followers and viewers.

I would also recommend you to provide something like a customer service platform.
But,

Don't forget to prioritise your goals.

Choosing the Social Networks

You will have to decide which Social network is relevant to which section of audience.

Just don't randomly set up profiles on each network.it is a very wrong way of your social media Strategy.

You must carefully choose your social networks observing how you can reach your maximum audience.

You can also grow your reach on more platforms by proving the ROI of the networks you got started with.

Keep organised

Don't start tweeting yet! First it's important to define a clear social media execution plan.
If you're targeting different channels for different audiences, things can get complicated very quickly.
You should know which social media profiles go together, which pages on your site you should be linking to, and how all of your campaigns should tie together.

You will find the relevant tips in the following pages..

Have A Hub..

To keep things organised,you should define a blog or a forum or community page where all of your new content is posted for the very first time.

Write the blog or post in most commonly spoken language that segment of audience uses to communicate.

Link all the other social media tools and channels to the main content source that is the Hub.

The Hub should also be a key part of your SEO strategy.

Selection of social sites

Each target audience should be observed to identify which social sites they mostly use.

Based on the social site,you will create page and profile.

Don't create different profiles and pages for different set of audience as it will be very cumbersome.

To maintain multiple pages and profiles instead Just have a single page and profile.

Putting efforts in a single profile and page will get momentum and attract a much larger fan base thus making your marketing effort more successful.

Link the profiles

As you have made the required blogs and profiles, Now is the time to link them.

The linking should be done appropriately and Hub should be given utmost priority.

while linking as it is the main content source.

If you have used various profiles for different languages then link only the profiles resembling same language that is your English blog should be linked to the accounts where you communicate in English only.

Viral marketing

The best thing about internet is when your idea takes off,instant fame and fortune are delivered for free.This BUZZ or word of mouth or blog marketing drives instant action .one person sends it to another,

In turn he sends it to another who shares it to others.

The challenge is to harness this word to mouth power.

I hope this section will help you learn more about making your ventures go viral on the world wide web.

The formula for success includes a combination of videos,blogentry,interactive tool and ebook adding to that a network of people who will light the fire and spread your links.

Gambling on campaigns and ventures

I recommend the marketers to always think like a venture capitalists or gamblers. Some of the strategies work while some fail.

While It is really difficult to create viral buzz, as a typical gambler or venture capitalist assume that most of you deals ,compaignsetc will fail but hopefully one will take off and become so big that it will repay you enough to make up for your losses and returning you many times your investment.

Movie studios etc follow the same principles expecting most of their projects will give them just enough to sustain but one hit will repay cost of a bunch of flops.

Nothing is sure to get Viral

I often come across agencies etc that they will charge money and in return create a viral campaign for you.

JUST DON'T GO FOR THEM!!

There are people who will tell you that it is possible to create a viral campaign that will
certainly be a hit, and there are agencies specializing in taking money and making promises.
But I've noticed that Vast majority of these campaigns fail.
.

I believe that it is impossible to create a marketing strategy or program with a guarantee that It will go viral.

Luck and Timing are always required .a huge amount of effort and dedication is also required

For example – consider a direct mail compaign.Do you ever check what it is about.98% of us don't even read it and directly send it to junk or spam while 2 percent are still there who will respond.

Our target is that 2% but for reaching that 2% we will have to send mail to 100% people.

So if you want response of 100 people, You will have to send around 5000 mails. Sounds easy??

Thank you,
For giving your precious time to this book.

Vardhane Harsh

Aknowledgements

This book wouldn't be possible without resources my parents and grandparents gave me .I would also like to thank my Teacher Mr. Benny Betrum for always guiding me on the path of morals and principles and motivating me to unleash my potentials.
Last but not the least I would like to thank all my friends who supported me everytime .

About the Author

Vardhane Harsh is the founder and managing partner of student organisation voithia based in chennai,India.The organisation helps students with internships ,project sponsorships and also helps NGOs to raise funds by various fundraising events. 19 year old Vardhane has passion for new age marketing and the same is reflected by techniques used to market voithia.Currently apart from running voithia,He is doing his mechanical engineering from vellore institute of technology chennai.

www.ingramcontent.com/pod-product-compliance
Lightning Source LLC
Chambersburg PA
CBHW071541170526
45166CB00004B/1506